Original title:
Carrying On

Copyright © 2024 Swan Charm
All rights reserved.

Author: Olivia Orav
ISBN HARDBACK: 978-9916-79-176-9
ISBN PAPERBACK: 978-9916-79-177-6
ISBN EBOOK: 978-9916-79-178-3

When Shadows Bow to Light

In the stillness of the dawn, we pray,
For hope to guide us on our way.
The shadows flee, their hold undone,
As morning breaks, and shines like the sun.

With hearts uplifted, we seek the grace,
In each trial, we find our place.
With every fall, we rise anew,
In faith, our spirits will break through.

The whispers of the night grow still,
With trust, we climb the highest hill.
For every tear that we have shed,
Brings us closer to the path ahead.

In the light, the truth is shown,
In love, we're never alone.
So let the shadows fade away,
And walk with us, O Lord, we pray.

When darkness comes, your light will guide,
Through valleys low and mountains wide.
We stand as one, our voices strong,
In the chorus of the timeless song.

As evening falls, our faith remains,
In quiet moments, we break chains.
For in your arms, we find our rest,
Forever held, forever blessed.

The Chronicle of the Faithful Journey

In the beginning, we took the road,
With heavy hearts, we bore our load.
With every step, we learn and grow,
In the hands of fate, our spirits glow.

Through storms we walked, through trials faced,
In trust and love, we found our place.
The road is long, the path is steep,
But in our hearts, the flame will keep.

With every tear, we sow the seed,
A harvest rich, to meet the need.
With courage found in lessons learned,
Our faith ignited, our hearts burned.

From mountain peaks to valleys deep,
We find the strength our souls can reap.
In every shadow, light will dwell,
In faith's embrace, all will be well.

The journey moves, the story flows,
As grace abounds, and love bestows.
With open hearts, we share the way,
In unity, we rise and pray.

So write this chronicle of our quest,
For in the trials, we are blessed.
Together bound, forever strong,
In faith, we sing our sacred song.

Unseen Threads of Courage

In quiet whispers, strength is found,
A heart that trusts, with faith unbound.
Through trials faced, we stand as one,
In shadows deep, our courage spun.

With every step, a path is laid,
In troubled times, our fears allayed.
Hands lifted high, to skies so vast,
We weave our dreams, the die is cast.

For in the dark, a light shall gleam,
Unseen threads connect, a sacred seam.
We break the chains that hold us tight,
With courage fierce, we claim our light.

Faith's Unyielding Flame

In hearts aglow, the fire ignites,
A beacon bright, through lonely nights.
Each flicker whispers, hope remains,
In storms of doubt, love breaks the chains.

Through every trial, our spirits rise,
A symphony sung beneath the skies.
With every dawn, new strength we find,
Faith's warm embrace, forever kind.

In every tear, a chance to grow,
The flame within, hearts overflow.
It lights the way, our souls unchained,
In unity, His name proclaimed.

The Covenant of Perseverance

With steadfast hearts, we walk this road,
A sacred bond, a heavy load.
In times of struggle, we hold tight,
Together strong, we share the fight.

Each promise kept, a treasure rare,
A whisper of love in every prayer.
Through valleys low, we lift our gaze,
In faith and hope, we sing His praise.

Our spirits joined, through trials vast,
In every moment, a truth steadfast.
Bound by grace, we shall not yield,
The covenant formed, our hearts revealed.

Light Beyond the Darkness

In every shadow, hope will rise,
With whispered dreams, we seek the skies.
A gentle hand through night's embrace,
In darkest hours, we find His grace.

With every heartbeat, new beginnings bloom,
A promise held beyond the gloom.
The dawn will come, our spirits soar,
For light eternal, we search for more.

Through every loss, a lesson learned,
In every soul, a fire burned.
With faith as our guide, we dare to see,
The light beyond, forever free.

The Light That Guides

In the silence of the night, we seek,
A beacon shining pure and meek.
It whispers softly to the soul,
Reminding us we're never whole.

Through the trials and the strife,
The light ignites our sacred life.
With every step, it leads us near,
Wiping away each pain and fear.

In the glow of morning's cheer,
We rise again, our hearts sincere.
For in the warmth of love divine,
We find the strength, the path align.

So let this light forever burn,
In hearts that wait, in hearts that yearn.
Each flicker guides, each ray provides,
A soothing balm as hope abides.

As stars above in twilight gleam,
Our faith ignites what we believe.
With grace we move, with purpose clear,
In the light that draws us near.

Faith's Steadfast Path

Upon the road where shadows play,
We walk in faith, we find our way.
Each step a promise, firm and bright,
Guided by love, empowered by light.

Through valleys deep where doubts may roam,
We carry hope, we call it home.
With every heartbeat, spirits rise,
Creating ties that none despise.

When storms may roar, and skies grow dim,
Our hearts still sing an ancient hymn.
For in the chaos, peace awakes,
Revealing all that love partakes.

The journey long, the path is steep,
Yet in our hearts, the faith we keep.
Together strong, we face the test,
Relying on the gift of rest.

With hands united, we reflect,
The grace that's found in deep respect.
On faith's steadfast path, side by side,
We walk with love, our souls our guide.

In the Shadow of Resolve

In the shadow where dreams align,
We build our hopes on love's design.
With steadfast hearts, we choose to stand,
In every trial, we clasp His hand.

Though storms may threaten, winds may howl,
We find our strength, we wear the cowl.
For in the night, His love abides,
Guiding us through the shifting tides.

Each whisper of resolve we hear,
Ineffable grace that draws us near.
With courage born from faith, we rise,
Illuminating the darkest skies.

Through every wound and every scar,
We discover just who we are.
In unity, our spirits soar,
A testament of love, evermore.

So let us tread with hearts of gold,
Embracing warmth in the bitter cold.
For in the shadow of resolve,
The heart finds peace, our souls evolve.

The Burden of Grace

In the weight of grace, we find release,
A gentle touch that brings us peace.
Though trials come to test our soul,
In grace we breathe, in grace we're whole.

With every burden that we bear,
The love of God is ever there.
In quiet moments, faith ignites,
Transforming pain to sacred lights.

The yoke of life may feel too strong,
Yet in His arms, we still belong.
With each soft whisper from above,
We're cradled close in boundless love.

Through valleys low and peaks so high,
His grace will lift us, makes us fly.
For every tear that falls in vain,
A promise blooms, life's sweet refrain.

So in the burden, let us trust,
That grace will guide, as surely must.
With every step in love's embrace,
We find redemption in our space.

Faith's Gentle Whisper

In the quiet of the night,
Hope takes flight, a calming light.
Softly it calls, a soothing sound,
In every heart its love is found.

Through the valleys, shadows creep,
Yet faith's promise, we shall reap.
With every tear, a lesson learned,
In gentle whispers, our souls turned.

When doubts arise like hidden fears,
In prayerful moments, dry our tears.
A strength unseen, yet deeply felt,
In faith's embrace, our spirits melt.

With every dawn, a new embrace,
Finding solace in His grace.
A candle flickers, warmth provided,
In faith's whisper, we are guided.

Let the world around us sway,
In faith, we find our steadfast way.
For in belief, we stand as one,
Embracing joy like morning sun.

In the Wake of Trials

In the storm, we find our might,
Holding fast, through darkest night.
For trials bend but do not break,
In every heart, the truth we stake.

When burdens heavy weigh us down,
Lifted by grace, we wear a crown.
Each struggle shapes our spirits bright,
In patience learned, we seek the light.

Through the fire, our souls refine,
In each challenge, love's design.
With every fall, we rise anew,
In the wake of trials, faith holds true.

Mountains loom, the path seems long,
Yet in weakness, we find our song.
In fellowship, we bear the strain,
Through every loss, we gain again.

So let us walk, hand in hand,
In the wake of troubles, firmly stand.
With hearts united and spirits high,
Together we'll reach the endless sky.

Beneath the Everlasting Light

Beneath the heavens, stars ignite,
A tapestry of pure delight.
In every moment, love's embrace,
Guiding us through time and space.

Our burdens shared, our hopes aligned,
In quiet moments, peace we find.
With whispered prayers, we seek the night,
Together we bask in sacred light.

For every dawn brings forth the day,
With gentle hands, He shows the way.
In trials faced and joys amassed,
Beneath His gaze, our fears are cast.

The road ahead, though fraught with care,
With faith as shield, we bravely dare.
In unity, our voices raised,
Beneath the light, we stand amazed.

Embraced by love, our spirits soar,
Together we've found an open door.
In the eternal, we place our trust,
Beneath the everlasting, we are just.

Climbing the Sacred Stairs

With each step, our spirits rise,
Climbing high toward the skies.
In faith's journey, hearts unite,
As we strive to seek the light.

The sacred stairs, they bend and sway,
Yet in struggle, we find our way.
With every gain, our faith enchants,
In trust we learn, in hope we dance.

Mountain paths may twist and turn,
In the ascent, our hearts will yearn.
For through the trials, blessings bloom,
On sacred stairs, dispel the gloom.

With every heartbeat, grace flows near,
In every climb, we conquer fear.
Together strong, we rise and care,
In love eternal, climbing the stairs.

Let us hold to the goal in sight,
As we ascend toward purest light.
In faith's promise, forever true,
On sacred stairs, we walk renew.

The Promise of Dawn

In the hush before the day,
Whispers of hope gently sway.
Light breaks through with tender grace,
A reminder of love's embrace.

Each shadow fades with the sun,
New beginnings have begun.
Birds sing sweetly in the trees,
A hymn carried on the breeze.

Clouds dissolve in the warm glow,
God's assurances lightly flow.
Promises resting on each heart,
Guiding us as we depart.

Feel the warmth upon your face,
In the stillness find your place.
Dawn reborn, a sacred sight,
Embracing all with purest light.

Hearts open, like flowers bloom,
Casting aside eternal gloom.
In the dawn, all fears are gone,
Celebrate life's endless song.

Seeds Bursting Through Soil

In the dark, the seeds do lie,
Waiting for the sun and sky.
With faith they push through the ground,
In silence, miracles are found.

Nurtured by the rain's sweet kiss,
They stretch upwards, seeking bliss.
With roots entwined, they grow strong,
In the cycle, they belong.

Each leaf unfurls with tender grace,
Reflecting the Creator's face.
Life springs forth, a vibrant dance,
In nature's arms, we find our chance.

Hope is woven in their thread,
From barren ground, all life is fed.
In unity, they rise and sway,
A testament that love's the way.

Through struggle, they find their worth,
A glorious rebirth on earth.
In every bloom, a promise stays,
New beginnings, forever blaze.

Through Tears, the Path Glimmers

In sorrow's hold, a heart may break,
Yet in the pain, new strength we make.
Through tears that fall, the light does creep,
A guiding star in moments deep.

Each drop a story, each ache a song,
In the struggle, we find we belong.
With every sorrow, grace unfolds,
A tapestry of love that holds.

Like rain that nourishes the ground,
Through trials, joy can still be found.
For every shadow, light will dance,
In suffering, we find our chance.

So let the tears fall, let them flow,
They're sacred waters, they help us grow.
In the dusk, the dawn will rise,
A faithful promise in the skies.

With faith as our unwavering guide,
We walk the path, with love inside.
Through tears we see the truth revealed,
In every heart, a wound is healed.

The Everlasting Embrace

In the stillness of the night,
Love wraps round, a glowing light.
A gentle touch, a whisper near,
In every moment, feel Him here.

With arms outstretched, the Spirit calls,
Through darkest hours, His kindness falls.
Each heartbeat echoes, love so vast,
In every breath, the die is cast.

Boundless grace that knows no end,
In every soul, He is the friend.
The warmth of faith, a soft return,
In every heart, a fire will burn.

Through trials faced and battles fought,
His presence felt in every thought.
An everlasting, sacred space,
In every life, His pure embrace.

So let us gather, hearts aflame,
In unity, we lift His name.
For in His love, we find our place,
A haven met, the highest grace.

The Quiet Strength of the Soul

In silence lies a power, profound,
A gentle whisper, profound and sound.
The heart, though troubled, finds its way,
In faith's embrace, it will not sway.

Roots grip the earth, though storms may rage,
The spirit writes each sacred page.
Each tear a blessing, each trial a light,
Guiding the weary through the night.

Mountains may loom, shadows may fall,
Yet hope arises, answering the call.
Every footprint on this path we tread,
Is inked in grace, where angels led.

A prayer is planted in every breath,
Defying doubt, defying death.
The quiet soul, a steadfast flame,
In the darkest hour, calls His name.

In moments of stillness, wisdom flows,
The heart's soft whispers, the spirit knows.
With every heartbeat, love unfolds,
The quiet strength, a gift of gold.

Echoes of Celestial Promises

Beneath the stars, a promise glows,
In every heart, a faith that grows.
Whispers of hope in the midnight air,
Celestial echoes, a sacred prayer.

Mountains high and rivers wide,
In the Lord's embrace, we shall abide.
The heavens sing of peace anew,
Every sorrow finds its view.

Raindrops fall like blessings divine,
Each moment a chance to intertwine.
From trials rise the songs we share,
In unity, we breathe the prayer.

The future sparkles, bright and clear,
With faith as our compass, we've nothing to fear.
Together we walk, hand in hand,
As promises echo across the land.

In the silence, truth unfolds,
In stories of old, each heart beholds.
We stand as one, under the same sky,
With every heartbeat, we shall fly.

The Dance of Perseverance

Step by step, we learn to sway,
In the dance of life, day by day.
With every stumble, we rise again,
Finding strength in loss, and joy in pain.

The rhythm of courage beats in our chest,
In trials we face, we are truly blessed.
With faith as our partner, we glide with grace,
Through shadows and light, we find our place.

A dance for the weary, a song for the bold,
In struggles we weave, our stories unfold.
With every heartbeat, the music calls,
In the dance of perseverance, love never falls.

Through tempest and storm, we bravely move,
In harmony's arms, our spirits prove.
A waltz of trust, a tango of grace,
In every step, we find our space.

United in hope, we twirl and spin,
In the circle of life, we rise within.
The dance of the faithful, both fierce and sweet,
In the arms of love, we feel complete.

Threads of Gold in Troubling Times

In troubled times, threads intertwine,
Golden strands of faith, a design divine.
Every struggle a stitch in our tale,
A tapestry woven, we shall not fail.

With hands outstretched, we gather near,
Lifting each other, casting out fear.
In shadows of doubt, a light breaks through,
The colors of hope, in every hue.

Through valleys of sorrow, we walk as one,
With love as our guide, our battle's begun.
A tapestry bright, each heart a gem,
Together we weave, we rise again.

The loom of life holds joy and pain,
Each thread a blessing, each loss a gain.
A masterpiece formed in the fires of faith,
In the art of survival, we find our grace.

In every moment, beauty unfolds,
In troubling times, we find threads of gold.
Together we stand, hearts held high,
In the fabric of life, love will not die.

Guiding Stars in Darkened Skies

In the night, we seek Your light,
Stars that shimmer, shining bright.
Through the shadows, hope we find,
In Your grace, our hearts entwined.

Whispers soft, from heavens high,
With every prayer, our spirits fly.
Guiding us through trials fierce,
With every love that You immerse.

Glistening rays, a sacred sign,
In Your presence, we align.
Lost and weary, we shall stand,
In Your name, united hand in hand.

Through the storms, our faith will soar,
Trust in You, forever more.
With each step, our spirits gleam,
As we journey toward the dream.

Hearts alight with sacred trust,
In Your wisdom, we are just.
Guide us, Lord, through every test,
In Your arms, we find our rest.

The Flame That Ever Burns

In the heart, a fire glows,
A sacred flame, the spirit knows.
Through the trials, it remains,
In its warmth, our hope sustains.

Brighter still, in darkest hour,
Filling souls with holy power.
Guiding paths through every storm,
In Your light, we feel the warm.

Relentless in its gentle sway,
Leading us along the way.
Though the shadows long may creep,
In Your love, our spirits leap.

From the ashes, life reborn,
In our hearts, a bright new dawn.
An everlasting candle's glow,
Through every loss, Your love we know.

Together, hand in hand we stand,
With an ever-burning brand.
In the quiet, we discern,
From Your love, the flame will burn.

Lanterns of Hope Lighting the Way

In the night, we lift our gaze,
Lanterns bright, through darkened maze.
Each flicker tells a tale of grace,
Illuminating every place.

In Your light, we find our peace,
With every glow, our fears release.
Guiding souls with gentle care,
Showing us, You're always there.

Through the valleys, shadows cast,
With Your lanterns, fear won't last.
In the journey, hope shall thrive,
In Your love, our spirits strive.

Through the trials, faith shall rise,
Lanterns soar beyond the skies.
Together, we will surely stand,
In Your light, we hand in hand.

Each bright flame, a promise true,
Every path leads home to You.
In the night, together we pray,
Lanterns of hope lighting the way.

The Breaking of Dawn After the Night

When the shadows start to fade,
And the darkness is delayed,
A whisper of hope, the sun will rise,
Bringing light to weary eyes.

Through the tears, a cleansing rain,
In Your mercy, we find no pain.
With each dawn, our spirits sing,
In Your name, new life takes wing.

Every morning, grace bestowed,
As the light begins to load.
In Your presence, shadows flee,
In our hearts, we're truly free.

Guide us through the coming day,
With Your love, we'll find the way.
Hope renewed with every light,
In Your arms, we find our might.

Though the night may come again,
We will rise and not descend.
For You are the breaking dawn,
After night, a brand new morn.

Heavenly Anchors

In shadows cast by doubts we find,
The light of faith, our hearts entwined.
With prayers like sails, we journey forth,
To shores of grace, our true rebirth.

Upon the waves, His whispers call,
In every rise, in every fall.
With heavenly anchors, we stand tall,
In love divine, we shall not stall.

Through storms that rage and tempests roar,
We grasp the hope that we adore.
In unity, our spirits soar,
To realms of peace forevermore.

In every tear, a lesson bold,
In every heart, a tale retold.
With faith as deep as oceans wide,
We find our strength in Him, our guide.

So let us walk on paths of light,
With hearts aflame and vision bright.
For in His hands, our dreams take flight,
In love's embrace, we trust the night.

The Spirit's Resolve

When shadows whisper doubts untold,
The spirit's flame, fierce and bold.
In silent prayers, we seek the way,
To conquer fears and greet the day.

With every challenge, every test,
In faith, we strive to give our best.
The spirit's grace, our sacred shield,
In trials faced, our hope revealed.

In humble hearts, His love ignites,
With every breath, we find our sights.
We rise from ashes, wise and true,
Renewed by grace in all we do.

So lift your voice, let spirit sing,
Embrace the peace that loving brings.
With courage pumped through every vein,
In unity, we'll break the chain.

For though the road may twist and wind,
The spirit leads, our hearts aligned.
With every step, we'll forge ahead,
In faith we march, where angels tread.

Silence and Solace

In quiet moments, peace descends,
Where whispered prayers and stillness blend.
The heart finds rest, the soul renewed,
In silence deep, we're gently wooed.

The world may buzz with chaos loud,
But here we stand away from crowd.
In solitude, God's presence near,
In whispered breaths, He calms our fear.

As night unfolds, the stars align,
A tapestry of love divine.
In every glance, in every sigh,
We feel the warmth, we know He's nigh.

So let us gather in this space,
To find the truth in His embrace.
With open hearts, we hear the call,
In silence, solace conquers all.

For in the stillness, we discover light,
A glow that guides us through the night.
With every breath, we find His grace,
In silence sweet, we know our place.

Walking the Sacred Way

With every step upon this ground,
We tread with purpose, love abound.
The sacred path, our hearts align,
In every moment, love divine.

Through valleys low and mountains high,
We walk in faith, with heads held high.
With every trial, we grow more wise,
In trust, we find the strength to rise.

For in this journey, side by side,
We'll face the world, our hearts as guide.
In service pure, we share the light,
Together bound, our spirits bright.

With grateful hearts, we sing His praise,
In every dawn, through endless days.
In every heartbeat, joy we share,
Walking the sacred way, laid bare.

So let us dance upon this earth,
In every moment, find rebirth.
With love and grace, we pave the way,
Toward brighter tomorrows, come what may.

The Lifting of Burdens

In shadows deep, we seek the light,
A guiding hand, through darkest night.
With whispered prayers, our hearts arise,
The weight we bear the Lord supplies.

His yoke is easy, burdens shared,
With faith anew, our souls prepared.
In trials faced, we find our peace,
From heavy chains, we seek release.

The path may wind, the road may bend,
With every step, the angels send.
Their gentle wings, they lift us high,
In divine love, we learn to fly.

So cast our cares upon His grace,
With trust, we find our rightful place.
For every ache, a purpose told,
In sacred arms, our hearts consoled.

Sheltered in Belief

A quiet trust, a sacred space,
In every trial, we find His face.
With faith as shield, we stand upright,
In storms of doubt, we find the light.

Beneath His wings, our souls take flight,
In whispered hopes, we find our might.
Through valleys low, our spirits soar,
His love encircles, evermore.

Our hearts entwined, by grace embraced,
In sacred bonds, we find our place.
Together strong, through thick and thin,
In unity, we rise within.

So let the world, with all its strife,
Be but a backdrop to our life.
For in His name, we dwell secure,
With faith unshaken, hearts made pure.

The Trust of the Wanderer

Upon the path, a wanderer treads,
With every step, where the Spirit leads.
Through mountain peaks and valleys low,
In trust divine, we learn and grow.

The road is long, yet hearts are light,
With love to guide through every night.
In searching souls, the truth revealed,
Through every joy, His grace is sealed.

From shores unseen to desert sand,
In every trial, we take His hand.
With weary feet, the journey long,
In faith we find our voice, our song.

So wander on, with hope ablaze,
By sacred light, we lift our praise.
For every mile, a story told,
In trust, our hearts forever bold.

Songs of the Journey

In every heartbeat, songs arise,
A melody of deep, sweet sighs.
With hymns of joy and cries of pain,
Our spirits dance in life's refrain.

Through trials faced and mountains climbed,
With every step, we're intertwined.
The journey etched upon our soul,
In sacred notes, we find our whole.

With gratitude sung to the skies,
Each moment cherished, love never dies.
In every breath, the music flows,
A symphony that only grows.

From dawn of day to dusk of night,
The songs we sing, a pure delight.
In unity, our voices blend,
In harmony, God's grace transcend.

Hope Eternal Amidst Despair

In shadows deep where sorrows dwell,
A light breaks through, a whispered tell.
With faith, we rise, our spirits soar,
For hope's embrace shall rise once more.

When tears do fall and hearts feel bare,
We find the strength in fervent prayer.
In darkest nights, a dawn will break,
Reviving dreams, the soul's own stake.

Through trials fierce, we find our way,
With every breath, we choose to stay.
A promise made to those in need,
In unity, we plant the seed.

For in despair, we learn to see,
The light of love, the strength to be.
In every struggle, faith will gleam,
A river of hope—a sacred stream.

So let us walk this path so true,
With hearts ablaze, we shall renew.
In hope eternal, we shall find,
A solace deep, a peace aligned.

A Covenant with Tomorrow

In tender whispers of the night,
We seal our dreams with spirit's light.
With open hearts, we stand as one,
Embracing all that's yet to come.

The vows we make, a sacred bond,
To cherish life, to love beyond.
With faith in hand, we venture forth,
In search of joy, in search of worth.

Each sunrise blesses paths anew,
A promise held, a vision true.
Through every trial, together we stand,
A covenant forged, hand in hand.

Let kindness be our guiding star,
As we journey near and far.
With hope ignited, hearts ablaze,
We walk in grace through all our days.

Tomorrow beckons, vibrant, bright,
Our spirits lifted, taking flight.
In every heartbeat, this we vow,
To seek the good, to honor now.

The Unseen Guide Along the Way

In quiet moments, hear the call,
A whisper soft, the peace of all.
Through life's great maze, both wide and small,
An unseen guide is there for all.

When shadows loom and fears arise,
Look to the skies, the starry ties.
For in the dark, light's presence stays,
An unseen guide along the ways.

With every step and each concern,
We find the path, we swiftly learn.
In gentle nudges, there is grace,
The unseen guide, we embrace.

So trust the journey, trust the fall,
In every rise, in every call.
For love will lead, and hope will sway,
This unseen guide along the way.

And when we wander, lost and torn,
Know solace comes with every morn.
In every heartbeat, hear the say,
The unseen guide will light the day.

Trusting the Hidden Road

In faith, we tread on paths unknown,
With hearts alight, our spirits grown.
The hidden road may twist and wind,
Yet treasures wait for those who find.

With every step, we hold the dream,
In trust we walk, with love's sweet gleam.
Through thorns and trials, we will learn,
For every shadow, light shall turn.

When doubts arise and visions fade,
In quietude, our fears are laid.
The hidden road, a journey blessed,
In faith we march, the soul's own quest.

Let whispers of the heart unite,
To guide us through the darkest night.
With courage bright and spirits bold,
We'll trust the hidden road we hold.

In every stumble, grace will flow,
To heal the heart, to help it grow.
So together, we embrace the load,
In love we find this hidden road.

A Tapestry of Belief

In the loom of life, we weave our fate,
Each thread a prayer, each knot a state.
Colors of grace, shining so bright,
Together we stand, in faith and light.

In trials faced, our spirits soar,
With love as the guide, we seek and explore.
A tapestry rich, with stories untold,
In unity we gather, as hands fold.

Whispers of hope, in the gentle breeze,
A reminder of peace, that puts us at ease.
The fabric of trust, stitched by the divine,
Binding our hearts, in love we entwine.

In moments of doubt, when shadows creep,
We turn to the light, our faith we keep.
Each thread a commandment, we hold so dear,
Guiding our steps, year after year.

With joy in our hearts and hands raised high,
We celebrate life, beneath the vast sky.
In this woven tale, we find our place,
A tapestry of belief, draped in grace.

The Road of the Faithful

Along the path where the faithful stroll,
Each step taken is a glimpse of the whole.
We walk in light, through valleys and heights,
Trusting the vision that guides our sights.

With courage as our armor, we face each test,
In the arms of the divine, we find our rest.
The road may be rocky, with burdens to bear,
Yet love lights the way, in every prayer.

Through storms and shadows, we lift our eyes,
Seeking the dawn, where our hope lies.
In fellowship strong, we gather as one,
Journeying together, 'til the race is run.

With hearts entwined in a sacred dance,
We embrace the chance, the Spirit's romance.
In moments of silence, we hear the call,
The road of the faithful leads us through all.

For every step taken with trust and grace,
We find the blessings in every place.
So onward we walk, hand in hand as we go,
On the road of the faithful, love will always flow.

Threads of Devotion

In the quiet dawn, our hearts arise,
Threads of devotion, weaving the skies.
A tapestry formed of hopes and dreams,
In faith we gather, as sunlight gleams.

Each moment a stitch, a bond made tight,
Sewn with intention, in the sacred light.
Through trials we grow, in love we abide,
Threads of devotion, woven side by side.

Our voices united, a melody pure,
With trust as our anchor, we will endure.
With each gentle loop, a symbol of grace,
Threads of devotion, in every embrace.

In laughter and tears, we find our shared song,
In the fabric of faith, where we all belong.
Stitched by the Spirit, our purpose aligned,
Threads of devotion, forever entwined.

Let our hearts be a quilt, rich and diverse,
In the thread of devotion, we find our verse.
Together we rise, through shadows and light,
Guided by love, our spirits take flight.

Beneath the Halo of Hope

Beneath the halo, where dreams take flight,
We find our refuge, in the softest light.
A sanctuary blessed, by grace from above,
Wrapped in the warmth of unconditional love.

In the silence, we hear the whispers of peace,
A promise of healing, a sweet release.
With hearts wide open, we gather near,
Beneath the halo, we conquer our fear.

Each moment a blessing, a chance to renew,
In the circle of faith, where the spirit proves true.
The halo shining bright, our guiding star,
Illuminating paths, no matter how far.

With gratitude flowing, like rivers we sing,
Beneath the halo, our blessings take wing.
In harmony's embrace, we find our way,
Walking in hope, come what may.

Together we rise, through each ebb and flow,
Beneath the halo of hope, love will always grow.
In the garden of life, where faith will bloom,
We thrive in the light, dispelling the gloom.

The Sacred Resilience

In shadows deep, the spirit's light,
A flame that burns through darkest night.
With faith we stand, unbowed and strong,
We rise again, where we belong.

The trials come, like waves they crash,
Yet in our hearts, we find our stash.
Of love and hope, entwined in grace,
In every struggle, we find our place.

The mountains loom, yet we ascend,
With humble hearts, our souls we mend.
Through every storm, we lift our gaze,
To brighter paths, our spirits blaze.

In whispered prayers, we seek the way,
Through dusk to dawn, we find the day.
With every step, we claim the ground,
For in His arms, true strength is found.

So let us walk, a sacred band,
In every heart, the Lord's command.
With hands uplifted, bold and free,
In sacred resilience, we shall be.

Echoes of Endurance

In quiet moments, whispers rise,
Echoes of strength, beneath the skies.
Each stumble teaches, each fall ascends,
With faith beside us, our path transcends.

Through trials faced, we learn to trust,
In every hardship, in Him we must.
He carries burdens we cannot bear,
With hearts united, we find our prayer.

Step by step, we journey on,
In darkness, light is never gone.
For every tear, there's joy bestowed,
In echoes of love, our burdens load.

Together we rise, hand in hand,
In unity's grace, we firmly stand.
Each whispered truth, a guiding star,
In echoes of endurance, near or far.

So let us sing through pain and strife,
In harmony, we find our life.
Each breath a testament, bold and bright,
In echoes of endurance, we find light.

Cherished Steps Forward

With every step, the path reveals,
The purpose deep, the love it seals.
Through winding roads and lessons learned,
In cherished steps, our hearts are turned.

The past may weigh, yet we are free,
To dance with grace, to simply be.
In trust we walk, through night and day,
In cherished steps, we find our way.

Hand in hand, we lift our gaze,
In gratitude, our voices raise.
Through trials faced, we grow more wise,
In cherished steps, our spirits rise.

Each moment holds a sacred gift,
In every heartbeat, our souls uplift.
With faith as compass, love our guide,
In cherished steps, we walk with pride.

So let us tread on paths anew,
With every choice, be firm and true.
In God's embrace, our hearts rejoice,
In cherished steps, we hear His voice.

Beneath the Weight of Trust

Beneath the weight, the burdens press,
Yet in the silence, we find rest.
Through trials, trials, and lessons clear,
In trust we rise, banishing fear.

With weary hearts, we lift our cries,
To skies above, where hope never dies.
In faith unfurled, we seek the light,
Beneath the weight, we find our might.

Each faith-filled step, a courage found,
In sacred moments, we are bound.
Though shadows loom, we shall not stray,
In trust's embrace, we find our way.

The path is steep, the journey long,
Yet in His mercy, we're made strong.
Through every doubt, through every trial,
Beneath the weight, we rise in style.

Together we stand, hand in hand,
In love's great name, we take our stand.
With trust as anchor, we will soar,
Beneath the weight of trust, restore.

The Spirit's Undying Flame

In silence deep, the spirit glows,
A light eternal, gently flows.
Through trials fierce, it holds its ground,
A beacon bright, where hope is found.

With every breath, the flame ignites,
In darkest nights, it shines so bright.
The soul's sweet song, it sings so clear,
Guiding the way, dispelling fear.

Within its warmth, the heart takes flight,
Embracing truth, that sets us right.
In faith we stand, unshaken, bold,
The Spirit's fire, turns hearts to gold.

So fear not storms that rage and howl,
For in His grace, we humbly prowl.
With tender hands, He lifts our cries,
His love the balm, where healing lies.

In every trial, through pain and strife,
The Spirit's flame breathes hope to life.
Forever burned in sacred space,
The undying flame of boundless grace.

Grace Through the Tempest

When storms arise, and shadows fall,
Grace finds a way to break our walls.
Through wind and waves, our faith we'll share,
In every trial, His love laid bare.

The thunder rolls, the lightning strikes,
Yet in our hearts, His peace ignites.
We stand as one, though trials come,
Together strong, we call Him home.

Amidst the chaos, songs will rise,
A chorus sweet, that never dies.
For every struggle brings forth light,
In darkest hours, we find our sight.

So lift your eyes, O weary friend,
His grace will lead us to the end.
Through winds of change, our spirits soar,
In Him we find forevermore.

Each tempest faced, a bridge to grace,
With every storm, His love we trace.
Through trials shared, our souls entwined,
In grace, through tempests, peace we find.

In the Hands of Providence

In quiet trust, we lay our souls,
In hands of grace, He makes us whole.
Through every turn, in light and dark,
His guiding hand, a sacred mark.

In paths unknown, our hearts abide,
With faith unwavering by our side.
The clearer skies give way to storms,
Yet in the dark, His love transforms.

For every tear that wets the ground,
In grace, a purpose can be found.
He weaves the threads of joy and strife,
In every moment, breathes us life.

Through trials faced, we rise and fall,
His gentle whispers, our constant call.
Embracing all, our spirits soar,
In providence, we find our core.

So in His hands, we rest our fears,
For every joy, and all our tears.
A tapestry of love divine,
In Him, our hearts forever shine.

The Journey of the Pilgrim's Heart

Upon the road, the pilgrim walks,
In quiet thoughts, the spirit talks.
With each step forward, faith is found,
In every stone, a holy ground.

Through valleys low and mountains high,
The heart takes wing, prepared to fly.
In every shadow, light will gleam,
The journey made, a sacred dream.

With every challenge, courage grows,
In trials faced, the spirit knows.
Companions true, through thick and thin,
Together strong, we rise within.

Each lasting bond, a gift of grace,
As hands entwined, we share this space.
Through laughter shared and sorrows weep,
In love's embrace, our hearts will leap.

So onward still, the path unfolds,
With every moment, truth beholds.
The pilgrim's heart, forever free,
In journey's end, His face we see.

Hymns of the Unbroken

In stillness, we gather, hearts aglow,
With whispers of faith, our spirits flow.
Through trials and storms, we rise anew,
In the light of His grace, we are made true.

Each breath a prayer, in unison we sing,
United in purpose, our praises we bring.
The bonds of our love, forever strong,
In the arms of the Divine, we truly belong.

Through shadows of doubt, His light guides our way,
In the night of despair, He turns night to day.
With hymns of the broken, we mend and we heal,
In the heart of our faith, we find what is real.

As mountains may crumble, and valleys may part,
Our souls are uplifted, a sacred restart.
In the dance of the faithful, together we soar,
With hymns of the unbroken, forever we explore.

In the Heart of the Struggle

In the heart of our struggle, we find our might,
Each challenge a lesson, through darkness, the light.
We stumble and rise, our burdens we bear,
With faith as our armor, we learn how to care.

In unity forged, our spirits entwined,
With love as our guide, our hearts will remind.
Through battles we fight, together we stand,
In the heart of the struggle, the Divine holds our hand.

Each tear is a river, each joy a song,
In the tapestry woven, we all belong.
With courage and grace, we weather the storm,
In the heart of the struggle, our spirits transform.

With purpose unyielding, we march ever on,
In the depths of our trials, our strength builds upon.
In the heart of the struggle, we'll rise and we'll shine,
For together, dear souls, our spirits align.

Stones of Strength

From the depths of the earth, the stones we arise,
Worn by time's hand, yet reflecting the skies.
Each stone tells a story, a journey profound,
In the echoes of ages, our truths can be found.

With faith as our chisel, we carve out our path,
Transforming our trials, not fearing the wrath.
In the strength of the stones, we find our own voice,
Through valleys and crests, we proudly rejoice.

In the fabric of life, these stones intertwine,
Each moment a blessing, each heartbeat divine.
With stones of strength, our fortress we build,
In the warmth of His light, our spirits are filled.

For in every struggle, a stone we will lay,
Building a pathway to guide us each day.
With stones of resilience, we stand ever tall,
Through love and grace, we will conquer it all.

Pilgrimage of the Spirit

On the pilgrimage of spirit, we walk hand in hand,
Through valleys of doubt and the shimmering sand.
With faith as our compass, we venture afar,
Guided by the light of the evening star.

Journeying onward, each step we embrace,
In the tapestry woven, we find our grace.
Through trials and triumphs, our hearts finding home,
In the pilgrimage of spirit, we are never alone.

With the echoes of wisdom, we learn and we grow,
In the sanctuary of love, all worries we sow.
Every footstep a prayer, each breath a new start,
In the pilgrimage of spirit, we mirror His heart.

Through heights and through depths, our spirits entwined,

In the whispers of hope, our souls are aligned.
With faith as our journey, each moment we share,
On the pilgrimage of spirit, we walk in His care.

The Lifting of Veils

In whispers soft, the shadows sway,
A light unseen begins to play.
Veils of doubt begin to part,
Revealing truth that warms the heart.

With every prayer, a step bestowed,
Each tear once shed, a sacred road.
From depths of night, we seek the dawn,
In faith we rise, reborn, withdrawn.

The eyes of grace now pierce the haze,
Guiding us through this holy maze.
With lifted veils, our spirits soar,
United in love, forevermore.

In sacred silence, we rejoice,
The soul awakened, God's own voice.
With open hearts, we humbly seek,
In every word, He speaks to the meek.

So let us dance in pure delight,
Embracing all within His light.
Each veil that lifts reveals the way,
To endless joy in His embrace.

A Heartbeat of Hope Amidst Darkness

In shadows deep where silence lies,
A heartbeat stirs, the spirit cries.
Through trials fierce and doubts that cling,
Hope whispers soft, a sacred spring.

In darkest nights, the light is faint,
Yet faith remains, our hearts' true saint.
We cling to love, a beacon bright,
Leading us through the endless night.

Each moment fraught with heavy pain,
Yet still we rise, through loss, through gain.
Within our depths, a spark ignites,
A fire of courage that ignites.

From ashes gray, new life will bloom,
With every step, dispelling gloom.
In unity, our spirits blend,
With open arms, the heart will mend.

Embrace the hope that dwells within,
Let love untangle what's been pinned.
For in this life, we find our way,
A heartbeat of hope shall ever stay.

Journeys Beyond the Horizon

As dawn breaks clear, the journey starts,
With faith as guide, and hopeful hearts.
Each step we take, a choice to make,
To seek the truth, for love's own sake.

Beyond the hills, where dreams reside,
We walk with grace, in Him, we bide.
The horizon calls, a song so sweet,
A promise kept where hearts converge and meet.

Through valleys low, we shall not fear,
In every trial, He is near.
With every mile, our spirits grow,
In sacred trust, we come to know.

With fleeting sands, time slips away,
Yet in His hands, we find our way.
Each journey blooms, a tale to tell,
In every heartbeat, we dwell in well.

So onward, souls, to paths unknown,
With love as compass, we are not alone.
In journeys bold, let faith arise,
To touch the stars beyond the skies.

The Fortress of Faith

In trials fierce, the storm may roar,
Yet faith stands firm, a steadfast shore.
A fortress built on love divine,
Where shadows fade and light will shine.

In whispered prayers, our spirits rise,
With hearts entwined, we seek the skies.
Within this wall, a refuge found,
In sacred trust, we are unbound.

The winds may howl and darkness creep,
Yet in His arms, we safely sleep.
With courage born of strength above,
We walk in grace, enveloped in love.

Each stone we place, a story told,
Of battles fought, our hearts made bold.
Together strong, we face the strife,
Within this fortress, we find life.

So let us stand in unity fair,
With faith our guide, in every prayer.
A fortress raised, where hope will dwell,
In love and light, all will be well.

Watering the Seeds of Belief

In quiet hearts, the seeds do grow,
With faith as light, the whispers flow.
Nurtured in love, they find their place,
In every tear, a touch of grace.

The rain of hope, it gently falls,
Reviving souls, answering calls.
In moments frail, let courage rise,
For truth reveals, beyond the skies.

Together we stand, hand in hand,
As kindred spirits, we understand.
Each breath a prayer, each thought a plea,
In harmony, we strive to be.

With every dawn, new light we seek,
United in love, we find the weak.
Water the seeds with warmth and care,
A garden of faith, forever rare.

So let us tend this sacred ground,
Where hopes are planted, love is found.
By grace we grow, through storm and sun,
Watering seeds, our hearts as one.

Upon the Wings of Trust

Upon the wings of trust we soar,
In realms divine, forevermore.
Let shadows pass, our spirits rise,
Embracing light beneath the skies.

With every heartbeat, love it sings,
A melody of hope that clings.
Through whispers soft, we dare to dream,
In faith's embrace, all doubts redeem.

In trials faced, let courage stay,
With strength unyielding, we find our way.
Against the storm, our spirits bend,
In unity, we rise, transcend.

On gentle currents, hearts entwined,
We chase the truth that sets us blind.
For in our trust, the world awakes,
A tapestry of love it makes.

So let us soar on faith's bright wings,
Together we'll embrace what living brings.
In every heart, a glimmer shines,
Upon the wings of trust, divine.

The Unfolding Journey of the Spirit

In the journey of the spirit's flight,
Each step we take, a dance of light.
With open hearts, we learn to see,
The path of love that sets us free.

Through valleys low and mountains high,
In every sigh, a whispered why.
Yet still we walk, with faith in view,
For every shade brings colors new.

In solitude, we find our grace,
A silent song in sacred space.
With every heartbeat, wisdom flows,
A seed of truth that ever grows.

In trials faced, our spirits shine,
For growth emerges from the divine.
With every tear, a lesson learned,
In love's embrace, our hearts unturned.

So let us wander, hand in hand,
Through the shifting tides of fate's command.
The journey unfolds, ever bright,
The spirit's path, our guiding light.

The Eternal Embrace of Tomorrow

In the dawn of hope, tomorrow calls,
With tender arms, the spirit enthralls.
Each moment sweet, a promise made,
In love's embrace, we won't be swayed.

For every yesterday has shaped our way,
A tapestry of dreams in play.
With every star, a wish we weave,
In trust and grace, we learn to believe.

Together we stand, bold and free,
Embracing what the world could be.
Each heartbeat whispers of the new,
In every soul, a spark shines through.

So let us walk this path of light,
With hearts united, burning bright.
For in the embrace of tomorrow's grace,
We find our home, our sacred space.

With love as our guide, we shall endure,
In every challenge, we will be pure.
The eternal dance of fate we share,
In tomorrow's arms, forever fair.

A Chorus of Celestial Voices

In the glow of morning light,
Angels sing with hearts so bright.
Every note a prayer divine,
Binding souls in love's design.

Wings of grace, they soar above,
Carrying whispers of pure love.
With each hymn, a promise shared,
In their embrace, all souls are bared.

Stars align in rhythmic flow,
Guiding hearts where faith will grow.
On this path, we find our way,
In the light of God's array.

Through the trials that we face,
Voices rise, a sacred place.
Join the dance of hope and fear,
In the faith that draws us near.

With each tear, a seed is sown,
In the garden of our own.
Reaping joy from pain concealed,
In the love that is revealed.

The Sanctity of Unbroken Will

In the chambers of the heart,
Freedom blooms, a sacred art.
Against the storms, we stand so tall,
In our faith, we shall not fall.

Winds may rage, and shadows creep,
Yet through the dark, our spirits leap.
Stronger than the fiercest tide,
In each soul, a light abides.

Every doubt shall be a stone,
But in our will, we find our own.
With courage forged in sacred fire,
We ascend to reach higher.

When the path ahead is stark,
Hope ignites a steadfast spark.
In the valleys we will grow,
As unbroken spirits flow.

Let the echoes of our quest,
Find the strength in every test.
With hearts united, we shall rise,
Finding grace beneath the skies.

Manna from the Heavens

From the clouds, sweet blessings fall,
Nourishing the heart of all.
In each drop, a promise lies,
Grace bestowed from boundless skies.

Through the trials we have gained,
Lessons learned, the love sustained.
In the silence, whispers heard,
Every thought becomes a word.

In the wilderness, we seek,
Living waters, strong but meek.
With each meal, our souls are filled,
Hunger quenched, our spirits thrilled.

Let the faith become the guide,
On this journey, side by side.
Manna shared, our burdens light,
In the dark, we find our sight.

With each gathering, love unfolds,
Stories told, a warmth that holds.
Feast of love, our hearts ignite,
In His presence, pure delight.

The Altar of Endurance

At the altar, silence reigns,
In our hearts, we bear the pains.
Through the trials, a sacred trust,
In the dust, our souls adjust.

Hands held high in prayerful plea,
In our struggles, we are free.
From the ashes, hope will rise,
Guiding us to the skies.

Every burden, a heavy stone,
Yet through love, we are not alone.
With each step, our faith will bloom,
Lighting up the shadowed gloom.

Embers glow within the night,
Strengthening the weary fight.
In the distance, dawn will show,
What our spirits long to know.

On this altar, dreams are laid,
In the trust, our fears must fade.
Through endurance, peace we'll find,
In His grace, our hearts aligned.

Upon the Mountain of Hope

Upon the mountain, spirits rise,
Where faith like eagles soars the skies.
In valleys deep, the shadows fade,
With every prayer, a promise made.

The dawn breaks soft, a gentle light,
Whispers of grace ignite the night.
Each step we take, beholden true,
The mountain calls, our hearts imbue.

In silence, find what souls dare keep,
A sacred bond, in stillness deep.
Through trials faced, we learn to stand,
Together here, united hand in hand.

The winds may howl, the storms may rage,
Yet love prevails upon this stage.
With every tear, a seed is sown,
In hope's embrace, we're never alone.

As we ascend, our burdens light,
Guided by faith, our guiding light.
Upon this mountain, dreams awake,
A heaven's gift, for our hearts' sake.

The Well of Endless Faith

In the well of faith, we draw from deep,
A fountain pure, where blessings leap.
With every drop, a hope is born,
In darkest nights, a new day's morn.

The waters flow, in peace they sing,
A sacred truth, in everything.
Though trials rise, and doubts invade,
Our trust will bloom, it shan't degrade.

Each soul that drinks, finds strength anew,
In whispers soft, the spirit flew.
With hands uplifted, hearts align,
The well of faith, our hearts' design.

From depths within, courage flows,
In every heart, the promise grows.
No storm can shake, no fear confine,
This endless source, by love divine.

Together here, we gather 'round,
In unity, our voices sound.
The well of faith, our souls shall seek,
In every heart, the brave and meek.

Holding the Sunlit Path

Holding the path where sunlight gleams,
We walk with purpose, live our dreams.
With each new day, the light will guide,
In every heartbeat, love abides.

The way unfolds, with grace it flows,
A shining road where courage grows.
In laughter shared, in tears we mend,
Together we journey, hand in hand.

The sunlit path, where shadows fade,
In joy and sorrows, memories made.
With faith as our compass, we shall trust,
In every step, a bond robust.

Through valleys low, and mountains high,
We seek the truth that does not die.
The radiant light that leads us on,
In every dusk, behold the dawn.

As we hold fast, our spirits soar,
On this sunlit path, forevermore.
Companions dear, we walk in grace,
In love's embrace, we find our place.

Emblems of Strength in the Silent Struggle

In the silent struggle, strength is found,
Like roots that deepen in sacred ground.
With every trial, our spirits rise,
Emblems of faith beneath the skies.

Though storms may clash, and shadows loom,
In hearts of light, there blooms a bloom.
Each challenge faced, a story to tell,
In life's embrace, we learn to dwell.

With every heartache, wisdom grows,
In quiet strength, compassion flows.
Together we stand, in unity bound,
Emblems of courage, profoundly sound.

The weight we bear, a shared delight,
In darkness deep, we are the light.
Through every struggle, love's refrain,
An anthem sung amidst the pain.

So let us rise, and lift our eyes,
In silent strength, our spirits fly.
Emblems of hope, unwavering flame,
In the silent struggle, we'll proclaim.

The Pathway of Faithful Steps

Upon the road where hope doth lead,
Each footfall sings a gentle creed.
In whispers soft, the truth does bloom,
Guiding us forth, dispelling gloom.

Through trials faced, our hearts stay bold,
In every story, faith unfolds.
The light ahead, a holy guide,
With every step, we walk in stride.

In moments dark, the spirit gleams,
As love and trust fulfill our dreams.
Through patience learned and grace bestowed,
We find our way on this sacred road.

With every tear, a lesson learned,
In every turn, the heart has yearned.
To rise again, renewed in strength,
Our path of faith, a boundless length.

So hand in hand, we tread this way,
With prayerful hearts, we seek to stay.
In unity, we lift our song,
A melody where we belong.

Sheltered by Grace

Under the wings of love we dwell,
In quiet peace, our spirits swell.
With open arms, the grace descends,
A solace sure that never ends.

In storms of life that rage and roar,
We find our refuge evermore.
The gentle touch that calms the strife,
In every heartbeat, the pulse of life.

Though shadows loom, we fear no night,
For in His arms, we find the light.
With faith unshaken, we embrace
The warm embrace of boundless grace.

In whispered prayers, our hopes take flight,
The Spirit guides us day and night.
With grateful hearts, we sing His praise,
Forever sheltered by His grace.

So let us walk with heads held high,
In every breath, a heartfelt sigh.
For in His name, we stand as one,
Sheltered by grace, our journey's begun.

Songs of the Unyielding Spirit

In battle's fray, our voices rise,
With faith as armor, we reach for the skies.
The spirit bold, unbroken, strong,
In joyous chords, we sing our song.

From valleys low to mountains high,
Our hearts entwined, we soar and fly.
United sweet, in love's embrace,
We share our hope with every place.

Through trials fierce, we hold our ground,
In every heartbeat, strength is found.
For victory lies within our soul,
An unyielding spirit makes us whole.

Through darkest nights and stormy seas,
We find our peace in whispered pleas.
Together we rise, together we stand,
Our songs a bridge, a guiding hand.

With every note, our dreams take flight,
In harmony, we find the light.
The spirit sings, a melody rare,
In songs of hope, we're free as air.

Through the Valley of Shadows

In the valley where shadows creep,
We walk with faith, in silence deep.
Though darkness looms, we won't despair,
For guiding light is always there.

With heavy hearts, we tread with grace,
Each step a prayer in this sacred space.
In trials faced, we find our way,
Through valleys deep, we shall not sway.

For every burden, a lesson learned,
Through steadfast hope, our spirits burned.
In trembling voices, we make our plea,
For strength divine to set us free.

The path, though steep, leads to the dawn,
In every setback, hope is reborn.
Through valleys dark, we hold the light,
To guide us onward, faithful and bright.

So trust each step, though fraught with fear,
In every shadow, love draws near.
Through the valley, we sing our way,
With hearts united, come what may.

Through the Doors of Suffering

In shadows cast by heavy hearts,
We seek the light that gently parts.
With each step on this weary road,
Hope whispers soft, a sacred ode.

Through trials deep, we learn to rise,
The spirit soars, it never dies.
With tears that cleanse, we face the dawn,
In suffering's grip, our souls are drawn.

A journey forged in pain and grace,
Each moment fraught with love's embrace.
In brokenness, we find our place,
To see the world through holy space.

Though darkness clouds our vision clear,
The light within will guide us near.
Through every wound, we find the bliss,
In the heart's ache, there comes His kiss.

Beyond the doors of lasting night,
Resilience fuels the soul's pure flight.
In every loss, a lesson gain,
Through suffering, we break the chain.

The Everpresent Hands of Grace

In moments when the world feels cold,
His gentle touch, a story told.
The hands that weave through joy and pain,
Assure us hope shall still remain.

With every breath, we feel His might,
Embraced by love, we find the light.
A guiding force in darkest hours,
His grace, a gift of blooming flowers.

Amidst the storms that shake our soul,
His presence makes us feel whole.
With faith as strong as ancient oak,
In every trial, His promise spoke.

The paths we tread, though fraught with dread,
Are graced by whispers of what's ahead.
In every step, we're not alone,
For He walks with us, His love our throne.

With hands extended, softly rest,
In His embrace, we are truly blessed.
The journey's fraught, but hearts won't stray,
In grace, we find our way each day.

Luminescence Through the Veil

Beyond the veil of earthly plight,
There shines a glow, pure and bright.
A glimpse of peace through worldly pains,
In faith, the heart forever reigns.

The sacred whispers through the night,
In solitude, we find the light.
The stars above, a guiding grace,
In every heart, a sacred place.

Through trials thick and burdens strong,
We sing our faith, a timeless song.
The luminescence, soft and clear,
Declares His love, always near.

In every shadow, hope will bloom,
Through darkened paths, dispel the gloom.
With eyes of faith, we gaze ahead,
Into the light where souls are led.

Beyond our fears, we take the leap,
In trust, our hearts are free to keep.
Through every trial, the spirit sails,
In luminescence, grace prevails.

A Tapestry Woven in Faith

Each thread a story, rich and rare,
A life adorned with endless care.
In color bright, our dreams entwined,
A tapestry of love designed.

Through storms we weave, through joy we thread,
In faith's embrace, our hearts are fed.
With every stitch, a prayer unspooled,
In sacred bond, we are all schooled.

From trials faced, the patterns grow,
Each tear and laughter, ebb and flow.
With hands divine, the fabric spun,
In unity, we are all one.

The whispers soft, in silence heard,
In gentle grace, we find the word.
Together strong, we rise and stand,
A sacred dance, hand in hand.

As seasons change, we still remain,
With faith our guide, we feel no pain.
For in this weave, a truth displayed,
In love's great tapestry, we're made.

The Unbroken Circle of Faith

In shadows cast by doubt and fear,
I find Your light, forever near.
With hands held high, I sing Your praise,
Through trials faced, my heart conveys.

The circle spins, true and divine,
In every moment, love aligns.
A bond unbroken, pure and whole,
In faith I stand, my spirit's goal.

With every step along this way,
I trust in You, come what may.
A journey marked by sacred grace,
In every breath, I see Your face.

The whispers soft, they guide my feet,
In paths of peace, my soul's retreat.
A unity that knows no end,
In You, dear Lord, I find my friend.

So walk with me through night and day,
Your love, my shield, in every fray.
The unbroken circle, binding tight,
Illuminates the darkest night.

Remnants of Grace in the Tempest

When storms arise and skies are gray,
Your grace, dear Lord, will light the way.
Through thunder's roar and tempest's might,
I find my calm, my heart's delight.

In every wave that crashes strong,
Remnants of grace keep me where I belong.
In trials fierce, I stand my ground,
In faith renewed, Your love is found.

With every tear, a lesson learned,
In sacred fire, my spirit turned.
Through howling winds, Your voice I hear,
A gentle call that draws me near.

The rain may fall, but hope shall bloom,
In gardens rich beyond the gloom.
A testament to strength and peace,
In every tempest, You release.

So let the storms of life descend,
In You, my heart will ever mend.
I carry forth the grace I feel,
In remnants bright, my soul shall heal.

The Sacred Bridge of Tomorrow

Upon this bridge of dreams we tread,
With faith alight, where hope is spread.
Each step a promise, each breath a prayer,
A sacred path beyond despair.

In whispered thoughts, the future grows,
With every end, a door that shows.
With love as guide, we walk anew,
In every heart, Your vision true.

Through valleys deep and mountains high,
The sacred bridge beneath the sky.
A pathway built on trust and grace,
Unfolding wonders we embrace.

The journey stretches far and wide,
With You, dear Lord, I shall abide.
In every step, my spirit soars,
For tomorrow calls, and hope restores.

So as we cross, hand in hand,
In unity, together we stand.
The sacred bridge will guide us through,
In every moment, I trust in You.

Wings of Resilience Above the Earth

With wings of faith, I rise above,
In every challenge, I feel Your love.
Soaring high on winds of grace,
In trials faced, I find my place.

The ground may shake, the storms may rage,
But in Your arms, I'll turn the page.
With every heartbeat, strength returns,
Resilience lit, my spirit burns.

Through valleys low and skies so wide,
I seek Your voice, my constant guide.
With wings unfurled, I face the light,
In every dawn, my hope ignites.

Your love, a current lifting high,
With every challenge, I learn to fly.
In courage born, my heart takes flight,
Above the earth, in purest light.

So let me rise, on wings of trust,
In every moment, I am just.
Resilience found in sacred worth,
I soar above, beyond this earth.

A Journey Through Trials

In shadows deep, we walk the path,
With faith as our guide, through pain and wrath.
Each step we take, the ground may shake,
Yet still our hearts, in hope, awake.

Through storms we face, and doubts that rise,
We seek the light, beyond the skies.
With every tear, a lesson learned,
The flame of strength, forever burned.

The road is long, with twists and bends,
Yet in the struggle, true strength transcends.
We carry on, with prayer and song,
For in His arms, we shall belong.

With faith unshaken, we rise above,
For trials teach us, the power of love.
United, we stand, hand in hand,
In the sacred light, we make our stand.

We find our peace in trust's embrace,
With every challenge, He gives us grace.
A journey blessed, through trials we'll tread,
In His name, our spirits are fed.

Ascending with Hope

Upward we climb, through valleys low,
With every heartbeat, our spirits glow.
On mountains high, our dreams are cast,
In faith we rise, our shadows past.

The dawn breaks bright, a new day sings,
With voices clear, the heartstrings ring.
In every struggle, in every trial,
Hope is the flame that lights our mile.

We seek the grace in every fall,
For in our weakness, He hears our call.
With lifted eyes, we chase the light,
In darkest hours, we find our fight.

His love sustains, through every storm,
In every challenge, His presence warm.
Together we tread, on paths unknown,
With trust in Him, we're never alone.

Each step we take, brings us near,
To a world of promise, free from fear.
Ascending with hope, hand in hand,
In faith we walk, on holy land.

The Whispering Promises

In the quiet night, a whisper stirs,
Soft as the breeze, the heart it purrs.
Promises made, in shadows' embrace,
Through gentle light, we find our place.

In every trial, the whispers call,
Through valleys of doubt, they break the fall.
"Fear not," they say, "for I am near,"
In every tear, He wipes our fear.

Each promise true, a guiding star,
Leading us forth from where we are.
In every heartbeat, in every sigh,
The whispers of hope, in the night sky.

With every dawn, their echoes rise,
Painting our dreams across the skies.
Through every struggle, they gently weave,
A tapestry of hope, we believe.

In faith we trust, the whispers flow,
Through darkest times, His love will grow.
In every breath, our spirits sing,
For in His promises, we find our wings.

Hands Lifted High

With hands lifted high, we praise His name,
In reverent joy, we play life's game.
In every moment, gratitude flows,
With hearts open wide, His love bestows.

In trials faced, we find our strength,
We gather hope, at faith's length.
Through every struggle, through every fight,
Our hands raised high, we seek the light.

With voices united, we sing as one,
In praises poured out, till day is done.
Each note a prayer, each song a plea,
In His embrace, we long to be.

For in surrender, we find our peace,
In trusting His ways, our worries cease.
With hearts ablaze, our joy ascends,
In love and hope, our message blends.

So let us rise, with hands held high,
Through every moment, we will not cry.
In faith we walk, in love we stay,
With hands lifted high, we find our way.

Threads of Light in Life's Weave

In shadows deep, we seek the thread,
A golden line, where hope is spread.
Each twist and turn, a story told,
In faith's embrace, our hearts behold.

From pain and sorrow, light does shine,
With every tear, a path divine.
We stitch our dreams in love's own hue,
In unity, we craft what's true.

The fabric worn, yet strong it stands,
Together woven, hand in hands.
In every stitch, God's mercy flows,
A quilt of grace, where blessings grows.

So let us weave through life's grand space,
With threads of light, we find our place.
Embracing colors rich and wide,
In every heart, His love abides.

Through trials faced, we see the light,
Each thread a sign, a guiding bright.
In faith we trust, with eyes refined,
Threads of connection, hearts aligned.

The Sustaining Breath of the Divine

In silence deep, His whispers ride,
As gentle winds, our souls beside.
With every breath, He fills the space,
The sacred air, our hearts embrace.

Awake, O spirit, rise anew,
In every moment, the breath comes through.
A sacred dance of give and take,
Each heartbeat sings, for love's own sake.

Through trials faced, our spirits soar,
In every breath, His grace restores.
With faith as anchor, souls align,
In unity, we touch the Divine.

Let not life's chaos dim the flare,
For in despair, He's always there.
A breath of life, a heartbeat's call,
In every moment, He holds all.

So take a breath, and feel His grace,
In every breath, behold His face.
The sustaining breath, forever near,
In love's embrace, we banish fear.

Resurrection of the Spirit Within

From ashes rise, a light once dim,
With every loss, we learn to swim.
In darkness deep, a spark ignites,
The spirit wakes, in resurrection's sights.

In trials faced, we shed our skin,
The old must go, the new begins.
With faith as guide, we journey forth,
Embracing life, we find our worth.

The dawn will break, as shadows flee,
New visions born, for all to see.
An inner strength, we now invoke,
With love's own light, our spirits spoke.

Through valleys low, and mountains high,
The heart beats bold, it learns to fly.
In every fall, we find our rise,
The resurrection, a sacred surprise.

So let us dance in life's embrace,
With open hearts, a smiling face.
In faith renewed, we take our stand,
Resurrection's song, a guiding hand.

The Steadfast Pulse of Belief

In quiet moments, faith takes root,
A steadfast pulse, our hearts pursue.
With every beat, we feel the spark,
A guiding light, dispelling dark.

Through storms that rage, we hold our ground,
In trust we stand, where hope is found.
Each trial faced, the spirit grows,
In strength we gather, love bestows.

With open hearts, we seek the way,
In every dawn, our spirits sway.
A melody of truth we sing,
In belief's embrace, the joy it brings.

The pulse of life, a steady drum,
In faith we rise, to what becomes.
Through every doubt, we find the grace,
A steadfast rhythm, time won't erase.

Together strong, we face the night,
In belief's warmth, we find our light.
A journey bold, our spirits lift,
The steadfast pulse, God's precious gift.

A Testament to Endurance

In the valley of shadows, we stand tall,
With faith as our anchor, we heed the call.
Through trials of fire, in darkness we tread,
For the light of His promise is never shed.

Each tear that we shed, a pearl in His sight,
Resilience our armor, in His grace we fight.
No storm can extinguish the flame deep within,
For the heart that believes shall always win.

With every heartbeat, a testament true,
In whispers of grace, we are made anew.
The footsteps we follow, in faith we shall roam,
For together in spirit, we find our way home.

When mountains arise, and tempests collide,
We lean on His promise, in Him we abide.
With courage and strength, we face the unknown,
In every adversity, we're never alone.

So let us proclaim, in unity's song,
That through every battle, our spirits are strong.
With hearts intertwined, we rise and ascend,
A testament forged, that with love shall not end.

The Covenant of a New Dawn

In the stillness of morn, a promise is made,
With shadows receding, a new light displayed.
The heavens rejoice, as the sun starts to rise,
The covenant whispers, in soft, tender sighs.

Each day is a gift, a chance to renew,
With faith in our hearts, we welcome the true.
The branches of hope stretch towards the sky,
In the garden of life, our spirits will fly.

From ashes we bloom, like flowers in spring,
The promise of grace, in our hearts we sing.
Through trials and changes, the soul finds its song,
As we walk in His light, we know we belong.

The night may be long, but joy comes in dawn,
With each step we take, in His light we are drawn.
We rise in the warmth of His whispers so clear,
The covenant alive, as we gather near.

In unity's embrace, we cradle the day,
With love as our guide, we will know the way.
A covenant cherished, in hearts we will keep,
As the light of His presence watches over our sleep.

Silent Prayers of Perseverance

In quiet moments, our whispers ascend,
Silent prayers echo, to Him we commend.
Each breath a devotion, a heart laid bare,
In temples of stillness, we find Him there.

Through valleys of doubt, with courage we stride,
In shadows, we gather, in faith we abide.
With every petition, a strength we reclaim,
In the silence we forge, we worship His name.

When burdens grow heavy, and hope seems unclear,
Our spirits unyielding, we draw ever near.
Through trials of fire, our faith like a flame,
In silent perseverance, we lift up His name.

Each tear that we shed is a seed in the ground,
In the soil of patience, new life shall abound.
The harvest of hope, our prayers shall unveil,
In the quietest moments, we shall prevail.

So let us not waver, in fervent belief,
For love is a fortress, our ultimate relief.
In silence we find, a love ever pure,
With silent prayers guiding, our hearts shall endure.

Blossoms of Hope in the Garden of Life

In the garden of life, where dreams take their flight,
Blossoms of hope bloom, bathed in His light.
Each petal a promise, each leaf a prayer,
In the beauty of grace, we discover our share.

Through seasons of change, we nurture the seed,
In faith, we plant love, fulfilled by our need.
With patience we tend to the roots intertwined,
In the garden of life, our hearts are aligned.

The sun paints the skies with a radiant beam,
In the hush of the morning, we gather and dream.
With every soft breeze, new blossoms will grow,
In the hand of the Creator, they flourish and glow.

As rain gently falls, washing sorrows away,
We gather together, united in sway.
With laughter and joy, we dance in the light,
In the garden of life, our spirits take flight.

So let us rejoice, for the harvest is near,
With love as the soil, we will not live in fear.
Blossoms of hope, in abundance shall thrive,
In the garden of life, we awaken, we thrive.

A Communion of Hearts

In the quiet of prayer we unite,
Souls intertwining in sacred light.
Hands raised in faith, a gentle caress,
A bond so pure, it knows no less.

With each whispered hope, we reach above,
Sharing burdens, spreading love.
Voices lifted, a harmonious song,
In this communion, we all belong.

Together we stand in the face of despair,
Finding solace in the love we share.
Hearts ablaze with a holy fire,
In unity, we rise, never tire.

Though trials may test our fragile might,
We walk together in the softest light.
For in this sacred gathering, we find,
Traces of the Divine intertwined.

As morning breaks and shadows flee,
A testament to hope, for all to see.
In the communion of hearts, we aspire,
To manifest love, and lift each higher.

Glimmers of Grace

In the stillness of dawn, grace appears,
Softly weaving through laughter and tears.
Each moment a gift, each breath a sign,
Illuminated whispers of the Divine.

Through trials we journey, we bend, not break,
Embracing the lessons that silence makes.
In shadows, we find the light that will guide,
Glimmers of joy, where faith will abide.

Nature's embrace in the rustling leaves,
Speaks of the comfort that love believes.
With every heartbeat, a promise made,
In glimmers of grace, our fears will fade.

In moments of doubt, remember the flame,
For each step we take, we honor His name.
With gratitude's song, we rise and we pray,
Glimmers of grace, our path, our way.

Let kindness abound in all that we do,
Reflecting the love that forever is true.
A tapestry woven with threads of light,
Glimmers of grace shining through the night.

A Path Beyond the Shadows

When darkness encroaches and doubts arise,
We seek the light beyond our sighs.
With faith as our compass, we journey on,
A path beyond shadows toward the dawn.

Each step we take, a whisper of hope,
In the tangled vines, we learn to cope.
Through valleys deep and mountains high,
We'll rise with wings as the eagles fly.

The soul's gentle yearning, a call to be free,
To glimpse the horizon, our destiny.
In trials faced, we gather our might,
A path beyond shadows leads us to light.

With prayers as our armor, we forge ahead,
Embracing each heartache, each tear we've shed.
Together in spirit, hand in hand,
We rise from the ashes, united we stand.

For in every struggle, a lesson we find,
A path beyond shadows, love intertwined.
So with courage we tread, with faith as our guide,
Towards the embrace of the Divine, side by side.

The Divine Embrace of Resilience

In the depths of despair, we find our worth,
A resilient spirit, reborn from the earth.
With every setback, our roots grow deep,
In the Divine embrace, our souls weep.

Life's turbulent storms may rattle our frame,
Yet through every struggle, we rise just the same.
With hope as our anchor and love as our sail,
The Divine embrace will never fail.

Through sorrow and joy, we journey as one,
Each battle we face, a promise begun.
In the whispers of faith, our strength is revealed,
The Divine embrace shall not be concealed.

We weather each trial, uplifted by grace,
Emerging with courage, we find our place.
In the heart of the storm, we dance with the flame,
The Divine embrace ever calling our name.

So let us rise high, like the phoenix reborn,
In this sacred embrace, we are forever adorned.
With resilience as wings, we soar through the night,
The Divine embrace guiding us toward the light.

Veils of Strength in Heart's Trials

In shadows deep where fears reside,
A light from heaven, our hearts abide.
With faith as armor, souls unite,
Through every storm, we find our light.

The trials come, like waves on shore,
Yet in His grace, we rise once more.
Each tear a prayer, each sigh a song,
In His embrace, we grow so strong.

The burdens heavy, yet we stand,
With whispers soft, He holds our hand.
In silent nights, His voice is near,
We walk in courage, free from fear.

When doubt surrounds like evening mist,
We lift our eyes, our hearts persist.
His promise true, through dark and fray,
A guiding star, our path each day.

With veils of strength, our hearts adorned,
In sacred love, we are reborn.
Through trials faced, we softly tread,
In faith we flourish, in hope we're fed.

Wrapped in Divine Assurance

In tranquil moments, hear the call,
A whisper gentle, love for all.
Wrapped in the arms of grace divine,
We find our solace, stars align.

Through valleys low, and mountains high,
His presence lingers, never shy.
With every heartbeat, trust we weave,
In sacred bonds, we dare believe.

The trials come like evening rain,
Yet in His hands, there's no more pain.
With every storm that shakes the night,
We stand in faith, embraced by light.

In silent woods, where shadows lie,
Our spirits soar, like birds on high.
Wrapped in His love, we shall not falter,
Each step we take, we rise, we alter.

The world may bend and hearts may break,
But in His truth, we shall awake.
Wrapped in His promises, we thrive,
In every heartbeat, we survive.

The Rooted Heart in Stormy Seas

Beneath the waves where chaos swells,
The rooted heart in silence dwells.
In stormy seas, our faith runs deep,
With every surge, His love we keep.

As thunder cracks and lightning flares,
We hold the line, for hope is ours.
Our roots like anchors, strong and true,
In turbulent times, we look to You.

With every gust, our spirits soar,
We trust the path that's worth the war.
The winds may howl, but faith shall steer,
In grounded grace, we persevere.

Through tempests fierce, our souls ignite,
In unity, we face the night.
The anchored heart will never part,
From love divine that fills the heart.

Come what may, we will not fear,
For in His presence, love draws near.
The rooted heart stands firm and whole,
In stormy seas, we find our soul.

Sacred Echoes of the Soul's Journey

In quiet whispers, truth resounds,
Sacred echoes in hallowed grounds.
With every step, His light we trace,
A journey witnessed by His grace.

The paths may twist, the shadows loom,
Yet in our hearts, there blooms a bloom.
With eyes wide open, we seek the dawn,
In sacred moments, we are drawn.

Through valleys low and mountains steep,
In faith, our promises we keep.
Each trial faced, a lesson learned,
In every heartbeat, love returned.

As sacred echoes softly call,
We rise in hope, we never fall.
With every breath, the spirit sings,
Awakening the joy He brings.

Our souls a tapestry, beautifully spun,
In sacred light, we're all as one.
With echoes strong, our voices soar,
On this journey, we are evermore.

Milton Keynes UK
Ingram Content Group UK Ltd.
UKHW021857151124
451262UK00014B/1322